THE WISDOM OF PAUL BRUNTON DAY BY DAY

PERPETUAL CALENDAR | DAYBOOK | BIRTHDAY BOOK
WITH PHOTOGRAPHS BY
CLASSIC VISION PHOTOGRAPHY

LARSON PUBLICATIONS FOR
THE PAUL BRUNTON PHILOSOPHIC FOUNDATION
BURDETT, NEW YORK

ISBN 10: 1-936012-29-4
ISBN 13: 978-1-936012-29-9

Cover: Moonrise, Matnuska Glacier
Title page: Geese and mist

Published by Larson Publications for
The Paul Brunton Philosophic Foundation
4936 NYS Route 414
Burdett, New York 14818 USA

larsonpublications.com
PaulBrunton.org

ABOUT THE PHOTOGRAPHER

On the first day of spring, the offices of the Paul Brunton Philosophic Foundation were graced with a most unusual communication. The proprietor of Classic Vision Photography, Haji Mahmood, wrote to invite a collaboration using his dazzling visual work, and quotes of Paul Brunton (PB). He included a couple of links to websites of his extensive library of work, and offered any and all of it for such use, explaining that PB's work had affected him deeply.

It was actually his 86-year-old aunt who talked him into contacting us, he later explained. He had completed a coffee table book for a popular celebrity, and his aunt commented that it was a beautiful and accomplished piece of work, but he really ought to do something with PB's writings! It was not really hard to convince him.

"I offer gratitude to him every morning on my 'sunrise rock' during my daily meditations," Haji told us in that first written communication. This revelation, along with his brilliant photographs, told us all we needed to know. Once we heard that and saw his dramatically moving work, we knew we would be working with him. This perpetual calendar is our first collaboration, and we hope there will be many more.

To learn more about Haji and his work, do explore his website: www.ClassicVisions.org

THE ILLUMINATING VISION OF PAUL BRUNTON

The illuminating words and ideas of Paul Brunton have inspired countless people from around the world over the last 80 years. From his earliest work, *A Search in Secret India* published in 1934, through the posthumously published *Notebooks*, he has delivered a comprehensive vision and practical guidance on life's meaning and value. He points us to a life path that delivers peace and wisdom inwardly and a life of richness and goodness outwardly.

There is an extraordinary power in the words of Paul Brunton, who became affectionately known as PB. Those of us who follow his dynamic pathway to Truth will find that our minds will be opened through reason and science, observation of our selves and our world, and we will come to see that all living beings live in a world manifest within our individual minds. Furthermore, we will find that all our minds are anchored in and inseparable from a Universal Mind, which is the source of all the laws of nature, of evolutionary unfoldment and of the radiating Goodness, Beauty, Grace, Wisdom and Love which guide us on our bumpy paths.

When PB speaks of the Divine Mystery, the Infinite Mind, we glimpse the peace and the power, the intelligence and the harmony that we find in our connection to It. He also shows us the many ways of living that help bring us to our true self, and to our own intimate relation to the Divine. He shows us how to overcome negative habitual sides of our nature and allow what is best in us and for us to flower. This helps us lead lives that bring forth the best that is in us and the best we can give to the world.

PB often demurred when pressed, and referred to

his work simply as "research." We reap the benefits of the profound depth and breadth of his inquiry into the mysteries of life and the universe, that he plumbed and was so expert at sharing.

The paragraphs in this book, along with the magnificent nature photos, depicting the mountains and all the sides of the natural world that PB so loved, give us a beautiful glimpse of what we find fully developed in the comprehensive volumes from which these words are taken.

To explore PB's vision further, turn to his published volumes (*a list appears on the last page*), or see the Foundation's website: PaulBrunton.org.

1

2

3

4

5

6

7

That out of which we draw

our life and intelligence is

unique and indestructible,

beginningless and infinite.

Open yourself in these silent periods to new intuitive feeling, and if it directs you to any new course of action, it will give you the power needed for that course.

8

9

10

11

12

13

14

15

16

17

18

19

20

21

You will sink into the profound silent depths of your own soul, yet you will never be able to say at any moment that you have touched the bottom. How could you? It is infinite.

The mind that is properly

used, and perfectly stilled

when not used, becomes

a mirror reflecting Truth.

22

23

24

25

26

27

28

29

30

31

1

2

3

4

You feel the Presence of something higher than yourself, wise, noble, beautiful, and worthy of all reverence. Yet it is really yourself — the best part come at last into unfoldment and expression.

It is this grandeur of self that is the magnetic pole drawing us to the Good, the Beautiful, the Just, the True, and the Noble. Yet itself is above all these attributes for it is the Attributeless, the Ineffable, and the Infinite that human thought cannot grasp.

5

6

7

8

9

10

11

12

13

14

15

16

17

18

The world is a spectacle

presented for our

meditation in depth.

It is a clue, a pointing sign,

and even a mystery play.

*What grander ideal could
a person have than to live
continuously in the higher
part of his or her being?*

19

20

21

22

23

24

25

26

27

28

29

1

2

3

When we come at last to
perceive that all this vast
universe is a thought-form
and when we can feel our
own source to be the single
and supreme principle in
and through which it arises,
then our knowledge has
become final and perfect.

The forming of a good character is the beginning, the middle, and the end of this work.

4

5

6

7

8

9

10

11

12

13

14

15

16

17

To enter this stillness is

the best way to pray.

Intelligence exercised
constantly in musing
upon the nature of life,
the movements of the
universe, the psychology
of humankind, and
the mystery of God — if
exercised in calmness,
intuitive balance, and
depth — leads to the
opening up of the soul.

18

19

20

21

22

23

24

LILY

25

26

27

28

29

30

31

The Overself is not merely a
pleasant feeling — although
it arouses such a feeling —
but a veritable force.
When it possesses you, you
are literally and actually
gripped by a dynamic energy.
A creative power henceforth
pervades your atmosphere,
enters your deeds, permeates
your mind and charges
your words, and runs through
your history.

That which we experience inwardly as thought must, if it be strong and sustained enough, manifest itself outwardly in events or environment or both.

1

2

3

4

5

6

7

8

9

10

11

12

13

14

The great elemental secrets
of life are so simple that
few see them. People are
complicated, intellects are
complicated, not life.

We need not become less human because we seek to make ourselves better people. The Good, the True, and the Beautiful will refine, and not destroy, our human qualities.

15

16

17

18

19

20

21

22

23

24

25

26

27

28

Those who weep in

their spiritual exile

do not weep in vain.

I am unable to separate
Life from God or the secular
from the sacred. I find a
divine element in all that is
brought forth by time.
But this is because when I
gaze deep within myself,
I first see it there, feel it there,
and commune with it there.

29

30

1

2

3

4

5

6

7

8

9

10

11

12

The mind has the power

to externalize the very

thing it perceives.

Lots of words are not needed to communicate what the Overself has to say. From its presence the truth, the power, and the virtue can make themselves felt.

13

14

15

16

17

18

19

20

21

22

23

24

25

26

These minutes spent in
utter unmoved stillness
can become a source
of great moral and
spiritual strength.

But the truth remains that
Nature holds us in her
grasp: there is no ultimate
escape. On some fated
day we shall all be called,
with an imperiousness
that will brook no dispute,
to our true home.

27

28

29

30

31

1

2

3

4

5

6

7

8

9

No one can see the Real

yet everyone may see

the things which come

from it. Although it

is itself untouchable,

whatever we touch

enshrines its presence.

In that silent centre

there is immense power

and rocklike strength.

10

11

12

13

14

15

16

17

18

19

20

21

22

23

It is a sweet peace gracious

beyond all telling.

*The laws of Nature remain
still unchanged even when
we find that Nature is
mental, and not material.*

24

25

26

27

28

29

30

1

2

3

4

5

6

7

Love is both sunshine for the seed and fruit from the tree. It is a part of the way to self-realization and also a result of reaching the goal itself.

The echoes of our spiritual being come to us all the time. They come in thoughts and things, in music and pictures, in emotions and words. If only we would take up the search for their source and trace them to it, we would recognize in the end the Reality, Beauty, Truth, and Goodness behind all the familiar manifestations.

8

9

10

11

12

13

14

15

16

17

18

19

20

21

And as this unifying spirit penetrates me more and more, a benign sense of well-being appears to be one result. I and all these friendly trees, this kindly earth, those white glistening peaks which rim the horizon, are bound up into one living organism and the whole is definitely good at its heart.

It is the power of imaginative thought, both human and deific, which produces the world-appearance for us.

22

23

24

25

26

27

28

29

30

31

1

2

3

4

Somewhere at the hidden core of our being there is light, goodness, power, and tranquility.

This is knowledge of
the highest order, that
everything around us and
within us, every bit of
Nature and creature, the
experience of life with a
physical body and of death
without it — all are but
forms of consciousness.

5

6

7

8

9

10

11

12

13

14

15

16

17

18

*This tormenting feeling of
the lack of a spiritual state
in your own experience,
will drive you to continual
search for it. But your
whole life must constitute
the search and your whole
being must engage in it.*

A life which contains no interludes of stillness can possess no real strength.

19

20

21

22

23

24

25

26

27

28

29

30

31

Just as a larger circle may contain a smaller one within it, yet the one need not contradict the other, so the ever-being of Mind may contain the ever-changing incredibly numerous forms of Nature without any contradiction.

THE WAVE, UTAH

The stillness has magical powers. It soothes, restores, heals, instructs, guides, and replaces chaos and tumult by orderliness and harmony.

1

2

3

4

5

6

7

8

9

10

11

12

13

14

*When these rare glimpses
are granted, take from
them as they leave all
that you can get — all the
strength, the wisdom, the
support, and the goodwill
that they can hold.*

Life is a dream,

an infinite dream,

without beginning

and without end.

15

16

17

18

19

20

21

SEPTEMBER

22

23

24

25

26

27

28

We experience the world

through the activity

of a Power greater

than ourselves, yet,

in another sense, it is

still our own activity.

If we could raise ourselves

to the ultimate point of

view, we would see all forms

in one spirit, one essence

in all atoms, and hence

no difference between one

world and another, one

thing and another, one

person and another.

29

30

1

2

3

4

5

ASPEN LEAVES

OCTOBER

6

7

8

9

10

11

12

*You now see what you
did not see earlier, that
the outer happenings
of your life are often
connected with the inner
trends of your thought
and that a change in the
latter will often produce
a change in the former.*

Our world is but a fleeting symbol, yet we may not disdain it. For it is the arched entrance under which we must pass through to the infinite life.

13

14

15

16

17

18

19

20

21

22

23

24

25

26

In its warm glow, people find a holy therapy for their suffering, a healing remedy for their disordered and dismembered selves.

Take up whatever path
is most convenient to your
personal circumstances
and individual character
and do not force yourself
into one utterly unsuited
to both, merely because
it has proven right for
other people.

27

28

29

30

31

1

2

EARLY SNOW

NOVEMBER

3

4

5

6

7

8

9

*Outwardly one's life
may suffer every kind of
limitation, from bodily
paralysis to miserable
surroundings, but inwardly
it is free in meditation
to reach out to a sphere
of light, beauty, truth,
love, and power.*

DEAD HORSE LAKE AND FOXTAILS

Each quest thus has its own character and its own personality. This it shapes by the act of dedicating itself to the incorruptible integrity of the higher life.

10

11

12

13

14

15

16

17

18

19

20

21

22

23

It is mind which makes

thoughts intelligible, things

experienceable, and the

thinker (the experiencer)

self-conscious — Mind!

the mysterious unknown

background of our life.

Within every single one of
us lies well upon well of
spiritual peace untapped,
of spiritual intelligence
untouched. From time to time
whispers come to us from
this second self, whispers
that urge us on to practise
self-control, to take the
higher path and to transcend
selfishness. We must heed
those whispers and exploit
those rare moments.

24

25

26

27

28

29

30

1

2

3

4

5

6

7

GEESE AND MIST

It is real, it is present and active in our very midst, its power and its guidance can be felt and recognized.

8

9

10

11

12

13

14

15

16

17

18

19

20

21

This habit of persistent daily reflection on the great verities, of thinking about the nature or attributes of the Overself, is a very rewarding one. From mere intellectual ideas, they begin to take on warmth, life and power.

From that high source of inspiration may come great actions, immense inner strength, superb artistic creativity, and a beautiful, delicate inner equilibrium.

22

23

24

25

26

27

28

29

30

31

The very essence of that Stillness is the Divine Being. Yet from it come forth the energies which make and break universes, which are perpetually active, creative, inventive, and mobile.

ABOUT THE PAUL BRUNTON PHILOSOPHIC FOUNDATION

The Paul Brunton Philosophic Foundation (PBPF) notes in its mission statement that Paul Brunton's (PB's) own mission statement might well have been "to promote the essence of spiritual development to all students of every faith and every social standing in language suited for the modern world," and the Foundation has taken this mission to its own heart. It further declares that the Foundation itself is "...dedicated to enriching the quest of every seeker..." PBPF was formed in 1986 as a steward first of PB's vast body of unpublished writing, and eventually, of most of his early works as well. In this capacity, the Foundation keeps *The Notebooks*, which it published, and early books, in print; creates new books; distributes both, free of charge, to target audiences such as prisoners and spiritual libraries; links study groups world-wide through international outreach; creates study guides and pamphlets based on PB's books; provides access to PB's ideas through the internet; is embarking on a massive archival project, and conducts various other activities. The Foundation aims to make the vision of PB and like-minded philosophers available to those who are interested in such ideas.

To explore further please visit the PBPF website: PaulBrunton.org

---

WORKS BY PAUL BRUNTON

A SEARCH IN SECRET INDIA
THE SECRET PATH
A SEARCH IN SECRET EGYPT
A MESSAGE FROM ARUNACHALA
A HERMIT IN THE HIMALAYAS
THE QUEST OF THE OVERSELF
THE INNER REALITY (DISCOVER YOURSELF)
INDIAN PHILOSOPHY AND MODERN CULTURE
THE HIDDEN TEACHING BEYOND YOGA
THE WISDOM OF THE OVERSELF
THE SPIRITUAL CRISIS OF MAN

PUBLISHED POSTHUMOUSLY

THE NOTEBOOKS OF PAUL BRUNTON
   (VOLUMES 1–16, CATEGORIES 1–28)
ESSAYS ON THE QUEST
MEDITATIONS FOR PEOPLE IN CHARGE
MEDITATIONS FOR PEOPLE IN CRISIS
WHAT IS KARMA?
A SEARCH IN SECRET EGYPT (ILLUSTRATED EDITION)